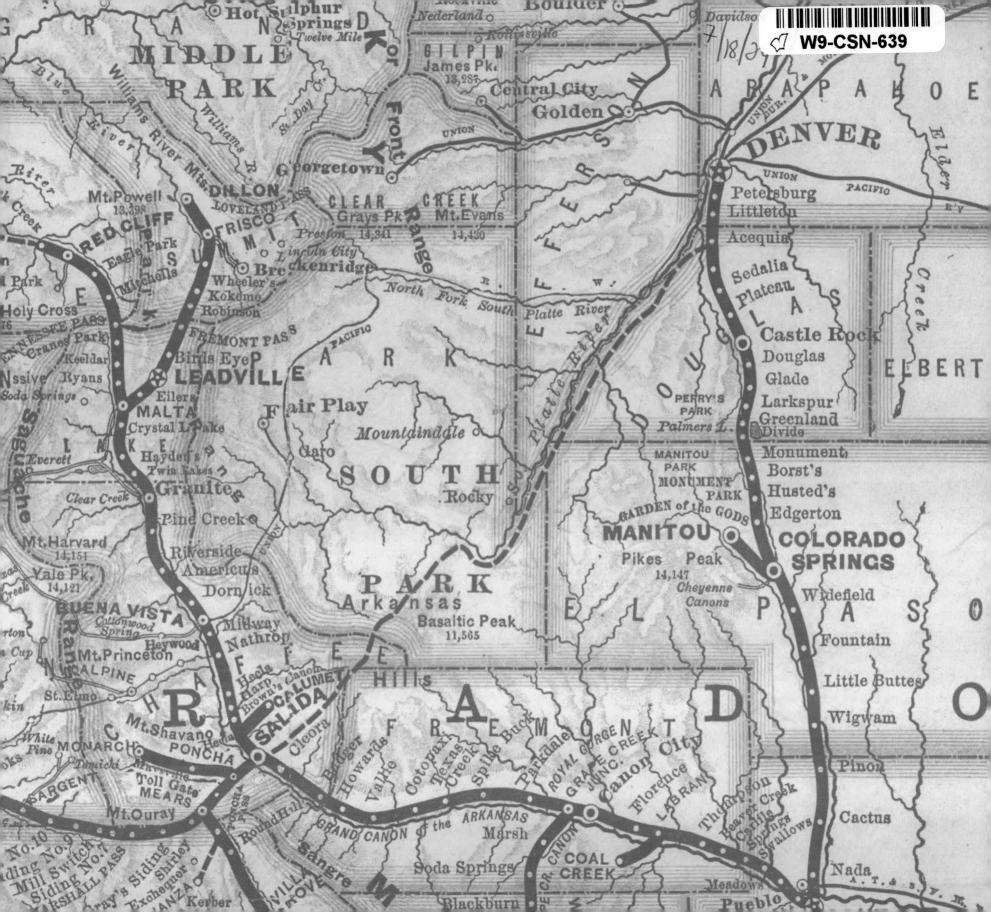

COLORADO
PAST AND PRESENT ™

COLORADO
PAST AND PRESENT ™

THUNDER BAY
P·R·E·S·S

San Diego, California

Thunder Bay Press

An imprint of the Baker & Taylor Publishing Group

10350 Barnes Canyon Road, San Diego, CA 92121

www.thunderbaybooks.com

Produced by TAJ Books International LLP

27, Ferndown Gardens,

Cobham,

Surrey,

UK,

KT11 2BH

www.tajbooks.com

Copyright ©2010 Taj Books International LLP

All notations of errors or omissions should be addressed to Thunder Bay Press, Editorial Department, at the above address. All other correspondence (author inquiries, permissions) concerning the content of this book should be addressed to TAJ Books, 27, Ferndown Gardens, Cobham, Surrey, UK, KT11 2BH, info@tajbooks.com.

ISBN-13: 978-1-60710-018-8
ISBN-10: 1-60710-018-5
Library of Congress Cataloging-in-Publication Data available on request
Printed in China.
1 2 3 4 5 14 13 12 11 10

The Publishers wish to thank Jennifer Vega, Rebecca Lintz, Jay DiLorenzo and their staff for their invaluable help with the historical images from the archives of the Stephan H. Hart Library at the Colorado Historical Society, and Greg Cox, archivist at Mesa Verde National Park. Special thanks to Thomas J. "Dr. Colorado" Noel, a Professor of History and Director of Public History, Preservation & Colorado Studies at University of Colorado Denver (UCD). The Publishers also wish to thank the numerous staff at the tourist offices throughout the state for their expert help and friendliness with this project.

CONTENTS

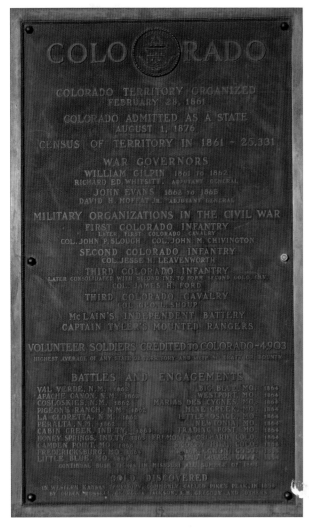

settlements offer a tantalizing glimpse of their day to day lives four centuries before Columbus arrived. One of the great archaeological mysteries is why they suddenly abandoned their apparently comfortable homes at the end of the 13th century and moved south.

Colorado is the historic homeland of many Native American tribes—the Cheyenne and Arapaho roamed the northeastern High Plains, Comanche and Kiowa hunted the southeastern plains, while the Ute Nation lived among the mountains and river valleys of the Rocky Mountains of Colorado. The Navajo eventually settled in southwestern Colorado, while the Apache moved through Colorado to the eastern plains. Modern Colorado has two Ute tribe reservations in the southwestern corner.

European invaders

Spanish conquistadors sent an expedition party led by Francisco Vásquez de Coronado north from Mexico in 1540; they were the first Europeans to see the high plains. They were specifically searching for the fabled cities of Cibola, where the streets were supposedly paved with gold. Without ever finding the cities, but still hoping, the Spanish claimed the land for their crown and kept returning for the next 250 years. The Spanish named the large river they found the Rio Colorado for the color of the red-brown silt it carried down from the mountains.

In 1682 the French explorer René-Robert Cavelier, Sieur de La Salle, claimed all the land east of the Rocky Mountains for King Louis XIV and France, even though he never set foot there himself. La Salle died in 1687, but his legacy of claiming lands for France became important in the early 1700s as the French began plans to colonize his claims, in part to counter the growing English dominance of the eastern seaboard as well as to expand their global holdings. The area which became Colorado was also coveted by the Spanish. In 1765, the explorer Juan Rivera led an expedition from Santa Fe (then Mexico, now New Mexico) northwards up the course of the Dolores River through Utah and Colorado in an attempt to find silver and gold, small deposits of which he did find.

History

The earliest inhabitants of Colorado were Native American hunter-gatherers who roamed across the plains and western plateau around 14,000 years ago. The earliest agricultural settlements started in about 5000 BC in the protected river valleys of eastern Colorado. It is thought these peoples learned about farming techniques from the Mississippi River Native Americans. Some of the most intriguing and mystical remains are from the highly sophisticated Anasazi culture who lived in multi-story cliff dwellings carved into the canyons of southwestern Colorado and still seen in the Mesa Verde region. Remains of these

◀▲ *Roxborough State Park southwest of Denver, about 15 miles south of the city of Littleton, is home to spectacular red sandstone formations.*

Louisiana Purchase and territorial acquisitions

Change started to arrive at the beginning of the 19th century when Spain ceded a vast area of southwestern North America, including eastern Colorado, to France on November 30, 1803. Only 20 days later Napoleon Bonaparte sold the same lands to the United States on December 20, much to Spanish indignation and fury. Bonaparte had originally wanted the western lands as part of his grandiose scheme to halt the western expansion of the U.S. and in the process increase the French empire. But trouble in the French West Indies forced French soldiers home to France, leaving no necessity for holding on to the western lands. Initially the U.S. only wanted New Orleans, but realizing that many Americans already lived and worked in the area (primarily trappers, hunters, and merchants), they bargained for the entire territory, which Napoleon suddenly agreed to sell them. In April 1803, for the total sum of $15 million, the "Louisiana Purchase" —including Colorado—became the property of the United States.

Exploration of the new U.S. lands in Colorado really started in 1806 when President Jefferson commissioned Lt. Zebulon Pike to reconnoiter the territory and covertly spy on Spanish positions. One of the sites he saw was a 14,110-foot peak, now named Pikes Peak after him; it became the symbol of the 1859 California gold rush to Colorado with the slogan "Pikes Peak or Bust." The expedition was arrested by Spanish cavalry in February 1806 in the San Luis Valley and taken to Chihuahua. They were detained for five months before being expelled from Mexico.

In the 1819 Adams-Onís Treaty, the U.S. gave up its claim to all the land south and west of the Arkansas River as part of the deal with Spain to buy Florida. But a few decades later following the Mexican-American War, Spain surrendered its northern lands to the U.S. in the Treaty of Guadalupe Hidalgo of 1848. The following year the Mormons of Deseret (now Utah) tried to claim all the land drained by the Green River and the Colorado River and declared the Provisional State of Deseret, but the U.S. government refused to recognize their authority. Instead, the land which would become Colorado was divided between the Territory of New Mexico and the Territory of Utah in 1850, and between the Territories of Kansas and Nebraska in 1854. At this point Colorado did not exist in any form.

Exploring the western lands

The newly acquired western lands remained a mystery, so in 1820 President Monroe sent Major Stephen Long, a government surveyor, to explore the southwest boundary of the Louisiana Purchase and report back on his findings. Major Long and his expedition worked their way up the South Platte River to the peak now named Longs Peak and made the first recorded ascent of Pikes Peak. The expedition was arduous, and when Long produced his map of the land, he called what was to become Colorado "the Great American Desert." The consensus was that the region was uninhabitable and virtually unfit for cultivation, with hardly any food or water. But Long did see the region as a barrier to western expansion and as a buffer against foreign invaders approaching from the west.

Fur trappers and traders moved their businesses to the Rocky Mountains in earnest in the 1820s, particularly in pursuit of beaver, which was highly sought after for fashionable fur hats. Beaver pelts commanded a good high price of up to eight dollars a pelt in the East. Famous names such as Ceran St. Vrain, Kit Carson, Louis Vasquez, Jim Baker, Jim Beckworth, William and Charles Bent, and Thomas Fitzpatrick made their living in the mountains. In the 1830s over 500 fur trappers roamed the Rockies trapping beaver.

Trading posts were set up where Native Americans would barter their goods: the most important of these were Bent's Fort (1833), founded by the Bent brothers and St. Vrain (near present-day La Junta) primarily for trading with Southern Cheyenne and Arapaho

Bear Lake, Rocky Mountain National Park. Sits at an elevation of 9,450 feet. The lake rests beneath the sheer flanks of Hallett Peak and the Continental Divide.

Bent's Old Fort National Historic Site features a reconstructed 1830s and 1840s adobe fur trading post on the mountain branch of the Santa Fe Trail.

Indians. During the 1830s, beaver was almost extinct in the Rockies and the fashion for beaver hats had faded; hunters turned to buffalo to make their living.

In 1842, "Pathfinder" Lt. John C. Frémont, one of the great explorers of the American West, accompanied by a party of around 35 men, undertook the first of five expeditions into the Rocky Mountains for the Army Corps of Topographical Engineers. While on a Missouri River steamboat, he met and became friends with Kit Carson, who he then engaged to guide him in the West. The subsequent Fremont Report published by Congress is credited with starting the emigrant wagon trail westwards.

Colorado was still virtually unknown at the time of the Mexican-American War and took little part in the conflict. About the only involvement was when General Stephen Kearney led the Army of the West along the Santa Fe Trail and passed through southeast Colorado on his way to take New Mexico from Mexico in 1846. By the Treaty of Guadalupe Hidalgo that ended the war, much of the land that Mexico ceded to the U.S. eventually became part of Colorado.

Gold fever

After gold was discovered in California in 1849, prospectors started looking elsewhere for possible deposits, and the Rocky Mountains looked like a good bet. In June 1851, the first permanent settlement in Colorado was founded at San Luis by Hispanic settlers from Taos; soon nearby Fort Massachusetts was built in the San Luis Valley to protect the settlers from Indian attacks. San Luis still holds an annual Fiesta de San Luis to celebrate the town's establishment.

In July 1858, a Georgia miner named William Green Russell disovered small gold deposits at the mouth of Little Dry Creek (now the Denver suburb of Englewood) and triggered the Colorado Pikes Peak gold rush of 1858-59 with its slogan "Pikes Peak or Bust." It has been estimated that between 50,000 and 100,000 prospectors rushed to Colorado hoping to make their fortune. Many of these fortune seekers were formerly farmers from the East caught by "gold fever" and completely ignorant of how to find and recognize gold. Many of them were even unable to pitch a tent, let alone cook and look after themselves in the wild. Amazingly, Russell and his brothers made a second gold discovery on Cherry Creek: Denver City was then founded by General William Larimer on the opposite bank of the Cherry Creek. Miners established two other camps in this area: St. Charles and Montana City. In 1860, the settlements merged and took the name Denver. Gold was discovered at other locations across Colorado, and this led to the establishment of more new towns such as Central City and Black Hawk.

In 1859, more gold was discovered at Chicago Creek (present-day Idaho Springs), and then a big strike was made by John Gregory at North Clear Creek attracting prospectors from across the nation and the founding of the camps of Central City, Black Hawk, and Nevadaville. With reports of each new strike, even more ambitious fortune-hunters flocked to Colorado and set up claims throughout the mountains, establishing mining camps at Tarryall, Boulder, Hamilton, and Gold Hill. Another significant strike was made in August 1859 at Blue River (present-day Breckenridge) by Reuben Spalding, but this proved short-lived and thousands of disappointed prospectors left for other areas within a year.

Colorado Territory

The Provisional Government of Jefferson Territory was proclaimed in October 1859 to administer parts of the Territories of Kansas, Nebraska, New Mexico, and Utah, lands which would become Colorado. The territory lasted for 16 months until the creation of the Territory of Colorado in February 1861. During its existence, the Jefferson Territory democratically elected government drew up rules and laws for the good governance of its lands with the intention of becoming a U.S. state in its own right. When President Lincoln was elected, Congress passed a bill organizing the Territory of Colorado instead. The census of that year gave the population of Colorado as 25,371.

Idaho Springs was formerly the gold mining town of Chicago Creek.

Black Canyon of the Gunnison National Park formed slowly by the action of water and rock scouring down through hard Proterozoic crystalline rock. In the 1800s, the numerous fur trappers searching for beaver pelts would have known of the canyon's existence, but they left no written record. The area was established as a U.S. national monument on March 2, 1933, and made into a national park on October 21, 1999.

In the 19th century, few settlers other than prospectors, hunters, and trappers made their homes in Colorado. Easterners looking for a new life in the western lands of Oregon, Deseret (later Utah), and California tended to avoid the difficult and demanding route through the Rocky Mountains of Colorado, preferring instead the easier, more northerly route following the North Platte River and the Sweetwater River through lands which would become Wyoming.

In 1860 when Abraham Lincoln was elected president of the United States, southern states seceded from the union in protest, and the specter of civil war loomed over the land. Needing to strengthen the hand of the free states (i.e., the non-slave states) the Republican-led Congress rapidly admitted the eastern part of the Territory of Kansas as the free State of Kansas in January 1861. This left the western lands, and crucially the gold fields, without government. Consequently, only 30 days later, on February 28, 1861, outgoing President Buchanan signed the act of Congress which created the free Territory of Colorado, and William Gilpin was appointed the first governor by President Lincoln. The boundaries of Colorado have remained unchanged since then. Colorado is one of only three states which has no natural boundaries (the others are Utah and Wyoming), only latitude and longitude borders. Colorado City was initially chosen as the administrative capital, but as the legislative assembly soon started to meet in Denver instead, the latter was named the permanent seat of the territory in 1867.

Native Americans and settlers

In the 1860s, Indian attacks against white settlers became more frequent as Colorado became more settled and the conflict of interests between the parties intensified. Native Americans, particularly Cheyenne and Arapaho, were increasingly pushed off their historic lands and were determined to fight back. The gold rush brought many new people to Colorado, much to the detriment of the Native Americans. In particular, the Pikes Peak gold rush brought matters to a head as Indians attacked wagon trains, stagecoaches, and mining camps.

Colorado governor John Evans wanted the Indians removed from much of their hunting grounds so white settlers could develop the land, but the tribes refused to be bought out and moved to reservations. The governor then called on Colonel John Chivington and his volunteer militiamen to stop the violence. Although a former clergyman, Chivington would mercilessly attack any Indian encampments he could find and kill as many Indians as possible.

Chief Black Kettle and his band of 600 or so Southern Cheyenne and Arapaho made their way to Fort Lyon and made their peace with the garrison there before camping at Sand Creek about 40 miles north. Chivington heard of their encampment, ignored the news of their surrender, surrounded their camp, and even though they were flying the white flag of peace and the American flag, pounded the encampment with cannon and rifle fire. Many Indians escaped, but between 150 to 200 men, women, and children were brutally massacred. Chivington was later denounced by a Congressional investigation and forced to resign. The atrocity ignited Native American resistance, and life in the remoter areas became even more dangerous for settlers and prospectors alike. More forts were built to protect travelers, such as Camp Collins (later Fort Collins).

Plains Indians undertook a campaign to drive settlers off their hunting lands on the eastern slopes of the Rockies. Indian attacks reached their peak in the mid 1860s, and the raids on wagon and supply trains pushed scarce food prices higher than ever: potatoes reached $15 a bushel and flour $40 for 100 pounds. Sioux and Cheyenne war parties using hit-and-run tactics destroyed settler villages and ranches, attacked wagon trains, and destroyed telegraph wires. In 1868, about 600 Cheyenne warriors led by Roman Nose were defeated at Beecher Island (near present-day Wray) by soldiers using Spencer repeating rifles. In 1870, the Denver Pacific Railroad started construction, and Colorado began to connect with the outside world.

Cheyenne scouts returning to camp. The Fort Laramie Treaty of 1851 granted the tribe northeastern Colorado, including what would become the cities of Fort Collins, Denver, and Colorado Springs.

Colorado National Monument. Independence Monument is all that remains of a continuous ridge that once formed a wall between Monument and Wedding Canyons. Near the city of Grand Junction, in the western part of the state, it is a semi-desert land high on the Colorado Plateau.

The Centennial State

Despite numerous attempts to join the union of the United States, Colorado Territory was denied statehood for 15 years. Finally in 1876, President Ulysses S. Grant signed a proclamation declaring Colorado the 38th state of the union. The new state was quickly nicknamed the "Centennial State" to celebrate one hundred years since the Declaration of Independence.

In 1878, a major discovery of silver near Leadville led to the Colorado silver boom. In total over $82 million worth of silver was mined, and much of it was bought by the U.S. government for coinage. The boom continued through the next decade and made many Coloradans wealthy, as well as enticing many newcomers into the state. The boom was further encouraged in 1890 with the passing of the Sherman Silver Purchase Act, which raised the price of silver to over $1 an ounce and was introduced to boost the ailing economy and particularly to aid the desperately debt-ridden farmers who were suffering from a long series of droughts. It also had the effect of encouraging further silver prospecting and mining operations.

The Sherman Silver Purchase Act increased the amount of silver the government had to buy each month to 4.5 million ounces. But the U.S. Treasury was required to buy the silver with promissory notes which could be redeemed for silver or gold. However, speculators and investors turned in their notes for gold dollars, and the government gold reserves were soon in danger of disappearing altogether. So, rather than having a positive effect, the result was inflation and a direct contributor to the economic panic of 1893. To stem the panic and preserve the gold reserves, President Grover Cleveland repealed the Sherman Silver Purchase Act in 1893, which brought about the collapse of the mining industry in Colorado, and in turn had a devastating effect on the agricultural economy of Colorado and caused enormous unemployment and deprivation across the state.

By 1900, the population of Colorado had risen to 539,700 (it did not reach one million until 1930), and gold was still being mined in quantity. Cripple Creek in Teller County was the second-richest gold-producing area in the world, mining $20 million annually, but despite this, pay and conditions for the workers and miners was very poor and led to violent strikes and property damage in 1903-4 when frustrations boiled over.

Modern Colorado

The Continental Divide runs through Colorado and across the top of the Rocky Mountains. All water on the western side drains westwards, ultimately towards the Pacific, and all water on the eastern side flows eastwards, ultimately towards the Atlantic. Colorado contains over 100 mountain peaks over 13,123 feet (4,000 meters) and none of the state is lower than 3,281 feet (1,000 meters), although almost half the state constitute the Great Plains. Colorado is still a relatively sparsely populated state, with most inhabitants living along the eastern edge of the Rocky Mountains. Colorado has one of the highest per capita personal income in the U.S. Agriculture, federal facilities, and military installations provide a great deal of employment, and Colorado is notable for its research and high-tech industries and healthy manufacturing base. In 1957, the North American Air Defense Command Headquarters (NORAD) was created between Canada and the U.S. and sited at a subterranean location underneath Cheyenne Mountain near Colorado Springs. In 1966 NORAD combat air operations opened its headquarters, also in Colorado Springs.

Colorado is rich in natural gas and oil as well as having substantial coal deposits. With its stunning scenery and natural beauty as well as ancient historic sites, Colorado is particularly rich with nationally protected areas. Tourism is a major business in Colorado, with visitors coming for the spectacular Rocky Mountains, the wonderful national parks, and of course, world-class skiing.

NORAD blast doors, Cheyenne Mountain, located on the southwest side of Colorado Springs.

Curecanti National Recreational Area. Three reservoirs, named for corresponding dams on the Gunnison River, form the heart of Curecanti.

STATE FACTS

STATE MOTTO

Nil Sine Numine is most commonly translated from Latin to mean "Nothing without Providence," although the intention of the original committee was to convey "Nothing without the Deity." It is most often seen as part of the territorial seal.

STATE NAME

Colorado comes from Spanish and means "colored red" and is a reference to the colors of the rocks and soils of Colorado. Congress chose the name Colorado for the territory in 1861.

STATE FISH

The greenback cutthroat trout (*Oncorhynchus clarki somias*) was indigenous to many small waterways across Colorado but suffered badly from pollution caused by mining and human occupation. In fact, it was thought to be extinct in the 1980s, but in the early 1990s small colonies were found living in remote Rocky Mountain streams.

McKee Springs petroglyphs.

STATE SEAL

Adopted in 1877, the seal is based on the one for the Territory of Colorado that was approved in 1861. The seal shows the eye of God inside a golden ray-emitting triangle, a scroll with the state motto, a bundle of birch rods and battle axe bound with red thongs (Roman fasces), and a heraldic shield showing snow-capped mountains over a pick and sledge hammer—miner's tools—and 1876, the year Colorado became a state.

Dinosaur National Monument. The rock layer enclosing fossils is a sandstone and conglomerate bed of alluvial or river bed origin known as the Morrison Formation from the Jurassic period some 150 million years old. Dinosaurs and other ancient animals were washed into the area and buried, presumably during flooding events.

STATE NICKNAMES

Colorado became a state in 1876, a hundred years after the signing of the Declaration of Independence, and so was nicknamed the "Centennial State." However, these days, the phrase "Colorful Colorado" is more often seen on tourist information centers, maps, and souvenirs.

STATE BIRD

The lark bunting (*Calamospiza melanocorys stejneger*) is a migrant bird arriving in April to spend the summer living on the plains before flying south in September. Male birds are black with white wing patches and edges, and white tail markings: this plumage changes in winter to gray-brown when they become difficult to distinguish from the smaller females.

STATE TARTAN

The pattern consists of blocks of forest green and cerulean blue separated by broad dividing bands of black; the green checks contain two pairs of lavender and white tram tracks: the blue checks contain a gold stripe with red guard lines. The tartan may be worn by any resident or friend of Colorado.

STATE FLAG

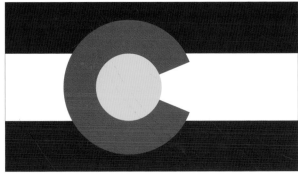

The flag of Colorado, adopted in June 1911, consists of three equal-width horizontal stripes of blue-white-blue. Slightly to left of center on the central white stripe sits a circular red "C," entirely filled with a central golden disk reflecting the state's gold mining origins and its three hundred days a year of golden sunshine.

◄▲ *Florrisant Fossil Beds National Monument. Beneath a grassy mountain valley in central Colorado lies one of the richest and most diverse fossil deposits in the world. Petrified redwood stumps up to 14 feet wide and thousands of detailed fossils of insects and plants reveal the story of a very different, prehistoric Colorado. The Adeline Hornbeck Homestead has been restored as part of the national monument.*

STATE SONG

"Where the Columbines Grow" by A.J. Fynn was written in San Luis Valley in 1896. While traveling by horse-drawn wagon to visit Native American tribes, Fynn was inspired to write his song by a beautiful Colorado mountain meadow covered with white and lavender columbines. He dedicated the song to Colorado pioneers. It became the official state song in 1915.

Where the snowy peaks gleam in the moonlight,
Above the dark forests of pine,
And the wild foaming waters dash onward,
Toward lands where the tropic stars shine;
Where the scream of the bold mountain eagle
Responds to the notes of the dove
Is the purple robed West, the land that is best,
The pioneer land that we love.

Chorus
Tis the land where the columbines grow,
Overlooking the plains far below,
While the cool summer breeze in the evergreen trees
Softly sings where the columbines grow.

The bison is gone from the upland,
The deer from the canyon has fled,
The home of the wolf is deserted,
The antelope moans for his dead,
The war whoop re-echoes no longer,
The Indian's only a name,
And the nymphs of the grove in their loneliness rove,
But the columbine blooms just the same.

Let the violet brighten the brookside,
In sunlight of earlier spring,
Let the fair clover bedeck the green meadow,
In days when the orioles sing,
Let the golden rod herald the autumn,
But, under the midsummer sky,
In its fair Western home, may the columbine bloom
Till our great mountain rivers run dry.

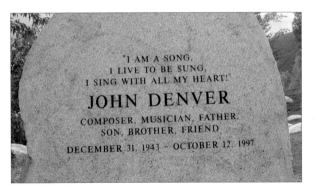

▲ John Denver's ashes were scattered over the Rocky Mountains in Colorado

SECOND STATE SONG

"Rocky Mountain High" by John Denver (lyrics) and Mike Taylor (music) was adopted in 2007. John Denver wrote the song about the beauty and wonder of the Rocky Mountains in 1972; initially there was a minor controversy as some people thought that it encouraged drug use, an allegation that Denver thought ridiculous.

He was born in the summer of his 27th year,
coming home to a place he'd never been before.
He left yesterday behind him
you might say he was born again,
might say he found a key for every door.
When he first came to the mountains
His life was far away
on the road and hanging by a song.
But the string's already broken
and he doesn't really care,
it keeps changin' fast, and it don't last for long.

Chorus
It's a Colorado Rocky Mountain high,
I've seen it raining fire in the sky
The shadows from the starlight are softer than a lullabye.
Rocky Mountain high . . . in Colorado . . .
Rocky Mountain high.

He climbed cathedral mountains, he saw silver clouds below,
saw everything as far as you can see.
And they say that he got crazy once and that he
tried to touch the sun,
and he lost a friend, but kept the memory.

Now he walks in quiet solitude, the forest and the stream,
seeking grace in every step he takes,
his sight is turned inside himself, to try and
understand, the serenity of a clear blue mountain lake.

Chorus
And the Colorado Rocky Mountain high,
I've seen it raining fire in the sky
You can talk to God and listen to the casual reply.
Rocky Mountain high, . . . in Colorado . . .
Rocky Mountain high.

Now his life is full of wonder,
but his heart still knows some fear,
of the simple things he cannot comprehend.
Why they try to tear the mountains down
to bring in a couple more.
More people, more scars upon the land.

Chorus
It's the Colorado Rocky Mountain high,
I've seen it raining fire in the sky
I know he'd be a poorer man if he never saw an eagle fly
Rocky Mountain high
It's the Colorado Rocky Mountain high,
I've seen it raining fire in the sky.
Friends around the campfire and everybody's high...
Rocky Mountain high, Rocky Mountain high,
Rocky Mountain high,
Rocky Mountain high.

◀▲ *Great Sand Dunes National Park. Alpine tundra, forests, massive dunes, grasslands, and wetlands are all protected as elements of the Great Sand Dunes natural system.*

STATE TREE

The Colorado blue spruce (*Picea pungens*) has a majestic, symmetrical shape and beautiful silver-blue foliage. It grows in small, scattered groves or singly among other species of pine. It grows in north Colorado at the elevation of 6,000 to 9,000 feet, while in the southern range between 8,000 to 11,000 feet.

STATE ROCK

Yule marble is a luminous white marble comprised of almost pure calcite grains. It has been used for numerous national monuments across the U.S. including the Washington Monument, the Lincoln Memorial, and the Tomb of the Unknown Soldier. It was first found in 1882 in Gunnison County on Yule Creek.

STATE REPTILE

The western painted turtle (*Chrysemys picta bellii*) is frequently seen around the wetlands of Colorado, but as its habitat is disappearing, its numbers are declining. Under 10 inches long, the carapace is brown or green with orangey-red borders; additionally it has orangey-red streaks on its limbs, head, and neck.

Rocky Mountain National Park. The park is located northwest of Boulder and includes the Continental Divide and the headwaters of the Colorado River.

STATE FLOWER

The Rocky Mountain columbine (*Aquilegia caerulea*) or Colorado blue columbine, is a pretty white-and-lavender-colored herbaceous perennial seen flowering in late spring and early summer. It was adopted as the state flower in 1899 and is a heavily protected species.

STATE GEMSTONE

Top-quality gem aquamarines are found in a small area 14,000 feet up in the high granite peaks of Mount Antero and White Mountain, Colorado. The crystals vary in color from light blue to pale or deep aquamarine green and can be up to almost 2.5 inches long. It was adopted in 1971.

Hovenweep National Monument protects six prehistoric, Puebloan-era villages spread over a twenty-mile expanse of mesa tops and canyons along the Utah-Colorado border.

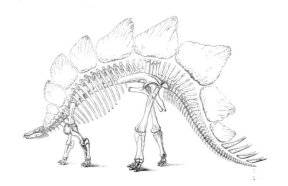

STATE FOSSIL

The Stegosaurus lived in Colorado 145 million years ago during the Mesozoic era of the Jurassic period, when Colorado was a vast lowland plain. The first fossil bones were found west of Denver in 1877 and many more have been found in Colorado since. The Stegosaurus was a 10-ton herbivore.

STATE GRASS

Blue grama grass (*Bouteloua gracilis*) is native to Colorado and found across most of the state. Blue grass grows across the vast North American prairies, where its dense, shallow roots hold down the soil and prevent it blowing away. The grass is a valuable resource important to the economic welfare of Colorado.

STATE INSECT

The Colorado hairstreak butterfly (*Hypaurotis cysaluswas*) is found on both sides of the Continental Divide at elevations of 6,500–7,500 feet in scrub oak ecosystems. The insect has black-bordered purple wings with orange markings in the corners, blue underwings, and a characteristic slender "tail" protruding from each hind wing.

STATE ANIMAL

The Rocky Mountain bighorn sheep (*Ovis canadensis*) is found only in the Rocky Mountains, usually above the timberline in rugged areas. It is distinguished by its magnificent curving horns. Although a large animal, it is remarkable for its agility and perfect sense of balance. The bighorn is protected from hunters by law.

STATE MINERAL

Rhodochrosite is a deep red to rose pink manganeze carbonate mineral found in some gold and silver ore-bearing veins in Colorado. The world's largest rhodochrosite crystal, called the Alma King, was found in the Sweet Home Mine near Alma (Park County), Colorado.

► *Lake Dillon in the Arapaho National Forest.*

▼ *Next spread:*
View from Colorado National Monument of the city of Grand Junction, the largest city in western Colorado.

FORT COLLINS

Fort Collins was founded as a U.S. military fort in 1864 on a previous settlement known as Camp Collins. It had been established beside Cache La Poudre River, which runs along the Colorado Front Range. Built during the Indian Wars in the mid 1860s to protect the new Overland mail route from Indian attack, Camp Collins was garrisoned by two companies from the 11th Ohio Volunteer Cavalry. Additionally, the camp provided a welcome respite for travelers on the Overland Trail until the site was destroyed by a flood in June 1864.

Numerous settlers built their homes near the security of the fort. It was decommissioned in 1867, the same year the town street plan was laid out. The first school and church had opened the previous year. In 1870, the Colorado Agricultural College was founded—it later became Colorado State University. In 1872, an agricultural colony was established at Fort Collins, and the town saw a population boom as hundreds of new settlers arrived and made their homes on lots just south of the original old town.

Fort Collins was incorporated as a town in 1873, but tensions between the early inhabitants and the new settlers caused political problems. The early economy of the town depended on stone quarrying, growing sugar beet, and sheep rearing and slaughtering. Beet tops fed the sheep, and, by the early 1900s, Fort Collins was known as the "Lamb feeding capital of the world."

Fort Collins grew steadily throughout the early 20th century, and, after World War II, the city was greatly modernized as

Panoramic view of College Avenue in Fort Collins, cars are by streetcar tracks, 1924.

long College Avenue today, the buildings are little changed, although the streetcar tracks have long since disappeared.

the population doubled. Colorado State University is located in Fort Collins and is the prime economic force in the city as well as the main cultural instigator. Between the late 1890s and 1969, the city forbade alcoholic beverages until the university students successfully protested against the ban. There is a now a thriving beer culture in the city. There are three microbreweries, the New Belgium Brewing Company, the Odell Brewing Company, and the Fort Collins Brewery. New Belgium is the largest of the local craft-breweries, with national distribution from California to states east of the Mississippi. The largest brewery in America, Anheuser-Busch, also has a suds factory in the city. There are several brewpubs, including the original C.B. & Potts Restaurant and its Big Horn Brewery and CooperSmith's Pub & Brewing, a local mainstay since 1989. The Colorado Brewer's Festival is held in late June annually in Fort Collins. The outdoor event is held in Fort Collins' old town area and features beers from as many as 45 brewers from the state of Colorado and averages around 30,000 attendees. Now Fort Collins has a high-tech economy with close links to the university but also a good balance of manufacturing- and service-based industries as well as many small businesses and ventures.

View of College and Mountain Avenues in Fort Collins (Larimer County), traffic includes horse-drawn buggies, wagons, and pedestrians, c. 1905.

oday's view of the same corner shows this building built in 1897, which used to house the Owl Drugstore, now home to Beau Jo's Colorado Style Pizza.

FORT MORGAN

Originally a military post called Camp Tyler, the settlement name was changed to Fort Wardwell in 1865, and then again in 1866 to Fort Morgan, after Colonel Christopher A. Morgan of the U.S. Volunteers. The fort was built to protect the mail service and pioneers moving along the Overland Trail. It was constructed by Confederate soldiers who had been released from prison on condition that they went west to fight the Indians. The soldiers also protected the Union Pacific Railroad builders and, when the latter's work was completed in 1868, the 1,200-man garrison moved to Fort Laramie, and Fort Morgan was destroyed—no sign of it remains today.

The area remained largely deserted until 1884, when Abner S. Baker started an irrigation project, and Fort Morgan became a thriving agricultural community producing livestock and dairy products and growing potatoes, sugar beets, corn, beans, alfalfa, and small grain. Agriculture still plays an important role in the economy, but the city also has significant manufacturing industries and an important international exporting base. Oil was found in 1950 in the nearby Denver-Julesburg Oil Basin, and refineries were built to process the oil; this in turn allowed local manufacturing businesses to become economically viable, making items such as irrigation pipes, hand tools, and concrete products. Now Fort Morgan has become a commercial and retail hub for northeastern Colorado. To the north of Fort Morgan lies Pawnee National Grassland and Pawnee Buttes. Called the "Sentries of the Plains," the buttes tower 250 feet above the surrounding grasslands.

View of the Masonic Temple on the corner of Main Street and Beaver Street in Fort Morgan (Morgan County). The building is a two-story brick structure with dentils, pediment frontispiece, arched doorways, and a Palladian window. Automobiles are parked in the street, 1927.

The Masonic Temple today shows the first-floor windows remain unaltered, but the ground-floor facade has been completely remodeled.

Two men sit in an open automobile near the Great Western Sugar processing plant in Fort Morgan (Morgan County). The factory is a three-story brick structure with large windows and a tall smokestack. A fourth story caps the building in two areas. A small, two-story brick office building is nearby, c. 1910.

December 2002, over 1,000 sugar beet growers in Colorado, Nebraska, Wyoming, and Montana united to form the Western Sugar Cooperative and finalize the purchase of Western Sugar from Tate Lyle. Western Sugar is Fort Morgan's largest single employer.

BOULDER

Boulder is situated in Boulder Valley where the Rocky Mountains meet the Great Plains, and to the east of the foothill stone slabs known as the Flatirons. The first Europeans to see the area were gold prospectors—when this was still part of the Nebraska Territory—who set up camp at Red Rocks near the entrance to Boulder Canyon in October 1858. Boulder Creek was named for the enormous granite boulders that fill the creek, which gets its water from the melting snows and small springs before joining the South Platte River. Within a year the Boulder City Town Company was organized with 56 shareholders, and the land was split into 4,044 lots, initially priced at $1,000 each (though later dropped to attract more buyers). The settlement grew slowly as a supply base and entertainment center for miners.

When Colorado became a state in 1876, the University of Colorado opened in Boulder after years of lobbying from the townspeople. In 1882, Boulder had sufficient population, with 3,000 souls, to become incorporated as a city. As with other Colorado towns, gold and silver mining were vital to the local economy, with later booms in coal and oil. Foreseeing the inevitable decline in prosperity, Boulder developed their tourist industry, which gradually took over as the most important element in Boulder's economy. The modern city of Boulder is surrounded by a greenbelt of city trails and open spaces. It is the home of the National Institute of Standards and Technology, which houses the new strontium atomic clock, with an inaccuracy of less than one second in 200 million years.

Bird's-eye view of Boulder: Courthouse on Pearl Street, University of Colorado's Hale Science Building (center left), Mt. St. Gertrude Academy and Chautauqua Park (center), and Flatirons (right); also shows wooden frame residences, picket fence, and outbuildings, c. 1920.

Boulder and the red-roofed University of Colorado from Chataqua Park. Considered a "Public Ivy," it is the flagship campus of the University of Colorado system and was founded five months before Colorado was admitted to the union in 1876.

Men, women, and children pose in front of an electric streetcar on 12th Street and Arapahoe Avenue in Boulder (Boulder County). Smokestacks are above a nearby building, probably a power house, June 24, 1899.

The National Center for Atmospheric Research's flagship Mesa Laboratory is located in the outskirts of Boulder, in a dramatic complex of buildings designed by architect I. M. Pei on grounds laid out by Dan Kiley. The surrounding grounds are maintained as a nature preserve.

DENVER

The biggest and most important city in Colorado is located in the South Platte River Valley on the High Plains near the Southern Rocky Mountains. Denver is popularly known as "Mile High City" because its official elevation is exactly 5,280 feet or one mile. Before the gold rush, inhabitants of the land were the Cheyenne and Arapaho Native Americans.

Denver was founded in 1858 as a mining town during the Pikes Peak gold rush. Early land speculators made money by laying out claims and then selling them to latecomers. One such, General William Larimer from Kansas, staked his claim overlooking the confluence of Cherry Creek and the South Platte River in 1858. He called the site Denver City after the Kansas territorial governor James Denver, hoping to curry favor with him, but he was too late, as Denver had already resigned. Then, in an attempt to establish a city and make his own fortune, Larimer sold parcels of land to miners and businessmen.

As a growing frontier town, Denver's economy was based on the local miners and their needs: gambling, saloons, livestock, and trading. Within a year (1859), there were three rival townships on both sides of the South Platte River, Denver City, Auroria and Highlands. In mid 1859, a big gold strike began at nearby Central City, and almost overnight Denver was deserted as the prospectors headed for the latest promised land. As quickly as it started, the Denver gold rush was over, but some of the fortune-hunters returned, as the harsh mountain climate proved too uncomfortable for them.

View of 16th Street in Denver; shows pedestrians, traffic, automobiles, a streetcar, and horse-drawn buggies and wagons, c. 1911.

The 16th Street Mall opened in 1982, originally from Market Street to Broadway, and was designed by Pei Cobb Freed & Partners. While I.M. Pei is often credited for the distinctive rattlesnake pattern found in the mall's granite pavers, Pei credits the design to his partner Henry N. Cobb.

Denver

Colorado Territory was created in 1861, and in 1865 Denver City became the territorial capital and shortened its name to just Denver. When Colorado joined the union in 1876, Denver became the state capital. In the 1860s and 1870s, the Union Pacific Railroad was built as the first transcontinental railroad, but its route missed Colorado. Well aware how much this would hamper trade and business growth, the people of Denver raised $300,000 and built their own railroad to link up with the Union Pacific at Cheyenne, Wyoming. Then, in the 1870s, the federally chartered Kansas Pacific Railway arrived at Denver just in time for the major silver strike at Leadville, bringing money and prosperity to Denver.

In 1863, a devastating fire burned much of Denver's business district to the ground. Then the following year, a flash flood ripped down Cherry Creek, causing millions of dollars worth of damage and killing 20 people. The city recovered and grew in people and business but also in corruption. Between 1880 and 1895, Denver was notorious for dishonesty as local politicians, police, and elected officials worked hand in glove with criminals. It was also the second-largest city west of Omaha for a few years.

In the early 20th century, Denver was one of many cities where engineers and designers worked on developing the automobile. Modern Denver is a big, thriving city and a major service and distribution center for the mountain states, while energy and mining groups are still important. In addition, many federal offices are located here.

A very muddy corner of Welton and 16th Streets, c. 1900.

Modern-day Welton Street is now home to numerous skyscrapers.

Denver Union Station was completed on May 13, 1881, to consolidate the numerous railroad depots around the city.

The same view of 16th Street from the Union Staion as it is today. Both corner buildings have changed little in over a hundred years, but unfortunately, the Welcome Arch was demolished in 1931.

"Mizpah" on the reverse of the Welcome Arch is a Hebrew parting salutation from Genesis 31:49: "The Lord watch between me and thee, when we are absent one from another."

ion Station is still served by Amtrak, and you can travel as far west as Emeryville, California, and as far east as Chicago, Illinois. The Regional Transportation District's light-rail whisks passengers to rious parts of the metro area.

People and horses stand beside an eroded Larimer Street during a flood of Cherry Creek in Denver. Note the brick and frame commercial buildings in Auraria and the flooded South Platte River, May 19, 1864.

Cherry Creek today, no longer a threat to the city that it once was. Placed in a high-walled channel, it has been landscaped, and a pedestrian and bike path has been added.

EVERGREEN

Onetime home of the Ute and Arapahoe Indians, the first Europeans to set foot in the region were French fur trappers, traders, and lumberjacks. The first settlement at what became Evergreen was a ranch built by homesteader Thomas Bergen in 1859, which also became a stage stop. Later, settlers built further south along Bear Creek, which is where the town grew up. In 1875, the settlement was named Evergreen by Dwight Wilmot, probably for the numerous perpetually green fir, spruce, and pine trees.

Evergreen's economy was propelled by the continuing demand for lumber used in building construction in Denver. By the 1880s, Evergreen contained six operating sawmills and had a population of 200 people. Further growth was stimulated by the improvement of the road from Denver up Bear Creek Canyon in 1911, and then the arrival of electricity service in 1917. Furthermore, with these two improvements, Evergreen started to become a popular summer destination for Denver residents, and many resorts opened to cater to the demand. Evergreen became quite fashionable and could boast many famous visitors, including both Presidents Roosevelt.

Until the 1950s, Evergreen remained relatively isolated from the outside world; increased ownership of the automobile enabled many people to move permanently to Evergreen, which became a commuter town for people working in Denver. Evergreen is surrounded by the Denver Mountain Parks and the Jefferson County Open Space.

A snowstorm on Main Street in Evergreen (Jefferson County), April 25, 1950.

This sleepy looking town has become a favored commuter town for Denver workers.

People ice-skate on Evergreen Lake in Evergreen (Jefferson County), c. 1930.

vergreen Lake Park includes a 40-acre lake, a park with picnic tables and grills, wetlands, an observation boardwalk, a 1.3-mile long trail, a historical boat/warming house. You can fish from sunrise sunset, but a Colorado fishing license is required.

GEORGETOWN

  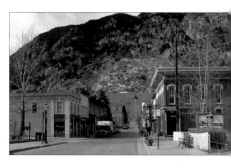

Located at the eastern base of the Snowy Range, Georgetown lies in the county of Clear Creek. The town was founded in 1859 by George and David Griffith, brothers from Kentucky who found gold in Clear Creek and decided to pitch camp there for a few months before winter. More prospectors arrived in the spring, and soon afterwards, the residents formed the Georgetown Company and claimed 640 acres on which to build their town.

The town remained quiet until 1864, when silver deposits were found eight miles up the canyon at Argentine Pass in the McClellan Mountains. Thousands of prospectors arrived, hoping to find their fortune as they dug into the mountainsides, and Georgetown benefited from their money. The town grew rapidly as a center for provisions, business, and entertainment for the miners.

In the 1870s, the narrow-gauge Colorado Central Railroad arrived, bringing with it more business and prosperity, and just in time to benefit from the Colorado silver boom of the 1880s, when Georgetown claimed to be the mining capital of Colorado (as opposed to its rival, Leadville). The town's population blossomed to over 10,000 but rapidly dwindled after the market dropped out of silver in 1893.

After its heady days during the silver boom, Georgetown became a quiet backwater. In the 1950s, it became a popular stopping-off point as an after-skiing watering hole between Guanella Pass and Loveland Pass. Small craft-type businesses started up, and by the late 1960s, Georgetown had become a popular tourist destination.

View of the intersection of Alpine (Sixth) Street and Taos Street in Georgetown (Clear Creek County). Dilapidated wood frame storefronts are on Taos Street. The Cushman Block, a three-story brick building with arched windows on the top floor, is on the corner, July 27, 1953.

The Cushman Block is still on the right-hand side in this image. During a severe snowstorm, the roof collapsed into the third story. When the building was repaired, owners converted it to a two-story building.

BRIDGE IN LOOP, W.H.J.&Cº.

View of Georgetown Loop Devil's Gate High Bridge in Clear Creek County, on the Union Pacific, Denver, and Gulf Railway Company line, includes two locomotives, five passenger cars, and a caboose atop the bridge. Clear Creek runs below the bridge's metal trestle supports. Photo taken between 1882 and 1900 by William Henry Jackson.

The Georgetown Loop Railroad is now a tourist attraction of the Colorado Historical Society. One can ride through the Rocky Mountains in an old steam locomotive that chugs up the Clear Creek Canyon. Departures are available from the Silver Plume Depot or Devil's Gate Station in Georgetown during the summer season.

LAKEWOOD

The now-large city of Lakewood was started in 1889 by Charles Welch and W.A.H. Loveland when they set out a 13-block area of Jefferson County in the foothills of the Rocky Mountains. The federal government purchased 2,040,207 acres (8.25642 km²) from the Hayden family in December 1940 for the purpose of building an ordnance (ammunition) plant, to be named Denver Ordnance. The site was chosen for its rural setting; because it was far from the nation's borders, it was presumed safer from enemy sabotage attack than coastal areas. In late January 1941, the War Department signed a contract with the Remington Arms Company to produce small-arms ammunition. Construction of the plant started in early March 1941. Rapidly, the government built over 200 buildings for the new Denver Ordnance complex, and ammunition production commenced in late September 1941. The plants were replaced by various federal agencies at the end of the war.

Lakewood was incorporated as a city in 1969 when it already had a population of over 90,000. It now has the fourth-biggest population in Colorado. Lakewood is near Arapaho National Forest and Roosevelt National Forest. Lakewood's economy is diverse, but the largest employers are governmental agencies. The Denver Federal Center employs about 6,200 people, and the Jefferson County R-1 school district employs 3,930. Gambro, a medical devices manufacturer, employs 1,654 people.

Cars jam the parking lot at the Denver Ordnance Plant (Remington Ordnance Plant, later the Denver Federal Center) in Lakewood, Jefferson County, c. 1941.

An officer in uniform stops to check a pickup truck at an entrance to the Denver Ordnance Plant (Remington Ordnance Plant, later the Denver Federal Center) in Lakewood (Jefferson County), c. 1941.

PARKER

When gold was discovered in Colorado in 1858, thousands of would-be miners arrived and scattered across the mountains in search of their fortune. In 1864, a one-room provision station was established by Mr. and Mrs. Long on a site at Cherry Creek; this became Parker. The building was known as the Twenty-Mile House as it was 20 miles from Denver; soon it became a 10-room inn where prospectors could reprovision, eat, lodge, and stable their animals and wagons. Twenty-Mile House changed hands several times and grew in size; in 1874, James Parker bought it, and soon Twenty-Mile House had a blacksmith, a general store, and the first post office in the area. Many of the early inhabitants of Parker were farmers of Scandinavian descent.

With the arrival of the Denver and New Orleans Railroad in 1882, Parker became more prosperous and soon had all the businesses and amenities of a thriving town. In time, the railroad became the Colorado and Southern Railroad, but after a series of financial disasters, its service wound down after 1913 and then parts of the track were dismantled in 1917. In common with other towns, Parker suffered during the 1930s Depression when low produce prices were insufficient to make a living, and even the bank was robbed. To make matters worse, the railroad was discontinued altogether after a disastrous flood in 1935 washed out many of the trestles. In the 1960s, after years of stagnation, people from Denver started to move to Parker, and the town began to grow rapidly. Modern Parker is now primarily a commuter town for Denver.

View of Seventeen-Mile House, a Smoky Hill South Trail stage depot at Cummings Ranch in Douglas County. Women sit and pose under the shade of a tree near a windmill. It shows a frame house, probably a barn in a field, and fences near a dirt road. Taken between 1890 and 1900.

Men, women, and children pose by a luggage cart at the Colorado and Southern Railway depot in Parker (Douglas County). Taken between 1890 and 1900.

MANITOU SPRINGS

This area was the traditional hunting lands and sacred grounds of the Ute, Cheyenne, Arapahoe, and other Plains tribes; they named the place Manitou, meaning "spirit." The nine named springs plus 15 others around the town are fed by the melting snows of Pikes Peak, which bubble up from deep subterranean aquifers with the rumbling noise of escaping gas. The waters sparkle with sodium bicarbonate and other healthy minerals, and each spring tastes different depending on the rocks it filters through.

In 1868, the area was surveyed by General William Palmer and Dr. William Bell; the latter, an English physician, recognized the area's potential as a health spa. The resort initially attracted tuberculosis sufferers, but was not really successful until the Denver & Rio Grande Railroad arrived in 1881 when a spur was built from Colorado Springs. Manitou suddenly thrived as thousands of visitors descended on the town. Soon, there were seven grand hotels, plus numerous smaller hotels, boarding houses, and summer rentals. Manitou was dubbed the "Saratoga of the West." Many celebrities visited, including the famous actress Lily Langtry, and fine restaurants and dance pavilions opened to cater to the demand. As the automobile became more accessible for ordinary people, the visitors started to arrive by car but only stay a few days before moving on. When the fad for mineral waters passed, Manitou drifted into gentle decline; then, in the 1970s, initiatives to revive the appeal of the springs were made. Neglected historic buildings were restored, and a thriving artists' colony started.

View of the Cliff House Hotel in Manitou Springs (El Paso County). The four-story frame building has a wrap-around open porch, balcony, dormers, bay windows, and awnings, c. 1900.

The Miramont Castle Museum is comprised of numerous architectural styles. These are used randomly throughout the four stories. For example, the grand staircase has two sets of windows, each in a different architectural style.

COLORADO SPRINGS

Colorado Springs was founded by General William Palmer in August 1871 as a tourist resort. It particularly attracted English visitors and so earned itself the nickname "Little London." The high altitude and dry climate also made Colorado Springs an ideal health resort.

General Palmer founded the Denver & Rio Grande Railroad to link his city to the wider world outside Colorado. He also wanted his town to be alcohol-free and accordingly bought up a huge tract of land east of Colorado City (now Old Colorado City), a place notorious for its brawling and saloons. Colorado Springs legally stayed alcohol-free until the end of Prohibition in 1933. Most unusually, Colorado Springs had its civic infrastructure (library, school, courthouse, etc.) built in stone on large, otherwise empty plots with wide streets already laid out before the influx of smaller businesses and houses. Much of the gold dug out during the Cripple Creek gold rush was processed at Colorado City ore mills, but the men who made their money out of the gold business did not want to live in such a rough town. Instead they moved to the more refined Colorado Springs and built themselves large houses on the undeveloped outskirts.

Colorado Springs started to grow as it became a tourist attraction, particularly for tuberculosis patients attracted by the mineral waters and dry climate. In the mid 20th century, Colorado Springs became a prime military location for the U.S. Army and the Air Force, bringing jobs, businesses, and wealth to the area. In 1942, the first military base was established in Colorado Springs on the

An 1890's view of Colorado Springs (El Paso County) shows wood frame houses, unpaved streets, and possibly schools and commercial buildings. The Rampart Range and Garden of the Gods are in the distance.

View of downtown Colorado Springs, as seen from Palmer Park. Colorado Springs is a home-rule municipality and is the county seat and most populous city of El Paso County. With an estimated population of 414,658 as of 2009, it is the second most populous city in the state of Colorado.

COLORADO SPRINGS

southern borders of the city, where the U.S. Army established Camp Carson for training horse troops for action in World War II. Nearby, the army began to use Colorado Springs Municipal Airport, which was soon renamed Peterson Field and used as a training base for heavy bombers. President Dwight Eisenhower chose Colorado Springs to be the location of the Air Force Academy. The military presence in the area brought military-related businesses and suppliers to Colorado Springs and greatly added to the city's prosperity. In 1951, the U.S. Air Defense Command moved to downtown Colorado Springs and opened Ent Air Force Base, which became home to NORAD between 1957 and 1963 before it moved to the high-security facility under nearby Cheyenne Mountain. Ent Air Force Base was closed in 1976 and became a U.S. Olympic Training Center. Thanks to the favorable climate and facilities, many U.S. sports have their headquarters in Colorado Springs. Meanwhile, Peterson Field became Peterson Air Force Base and the home of Air Force Space Command, and Camp Carson became Fort Carson and current home to the 4th Infantry Division and headquarters for parts of the 10th Special Forces Group. In 1983, Falcon Air Force Base (now Schriever Air Force Base) opened, and it is charged with prime responsibility for missile defense and satellite control. Because of its stunning setting at the edge of the Rocky Mountains, Colorado Springs also has an important tourist industry with many visitors wanting to see the famous Pikes Peak, soaring 14,100 feet high just west of the city.

A view of the Antlers Hotel in Colorado Springs (El Paso County) shows a seven-story building designed by Frederick J. Sterner with arcaded towers and balconies. The building has an arched entry with a terrace above and voussoir windows, c. 1901.

The Antlers Hilton Colorado Springs was originally built in 1883 and was rebuilt following a fire in 1901. The third rendition of this historic hotel was built in the 1980s.

CRIPPLE CREEK

Cripple Creek is the county seat of Teller County and was founded as a gold mining camp just below the timberline. The earliest inhabitants of the area were the Ute who lived on and around Pikes Peak in the summers and down among the lower hills in winter. The Utes slowly lost ground against the settlers and miners and eventually moved west onto two reservations, where they still live today.

The first adventurers to arrive were fur trappers after beaver in the early 1800s. When gold was found in the high valley in 1891, it started the last big Colorado gold rush. Between 1890 and 1910, 22,400,000 ounces of gold were extracted by around 50,000 miners from 500 mines in the Cripple Creek Mining District. The gold camp was served by three railroads and two electric trolley lines. The Florence and Cripple Creek Railroad ran 40 miles up the mountain from Florence three times a day until the track was washed away in 1912. The Midland Terminal trains ran 55 miles from Colorado Springs to Cripple Creek over Ute Pass four times a day until 1949. The Colorado Springs and Cripple Creek District Railroad, called the Short Line, started in 1901. Both electric trolley systems shut down in 1922.

Cripple Creek acquired a reputation as a decaying beauty and something of a ghost town. In the early 1990s, Colorado voters agreed to allow Cripple Creek to establish legalized gambling. The permanent population increased, and the casinos now occupy many of the once-empty historic buildings.

View of Bennett Street in Cripple Creek (Teller County) shows retaining walls, cars and stores, c. 1940.

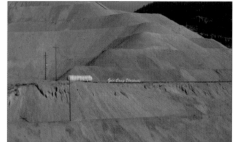

The exact same street today still retains the majority of its buildings, many of them now operating as casinos.

View of a brick warehouse and a frame horseshoeing business on East Warren Street in Cripple Creek (Teller County), 1904.

The Butte Opera House is a historic building that has been restored to Victorian-era splendor for music, theater, and community events. The Butte Opera House Foundation is a nonprofit corporation that supports events at the theater, including a year-round Community Theater Group and professional shows with local professional actors. The building is shared with the fire department.

VICTOR

Victor lies at the heart of Colorado gold country in the shadow of Battle Mountain, where the largest gold deposits lay. Gold was found in 1891 by Winfield Scott Stratton, who immediately started the Independence Mine. News of the strike brought thousands of miners and, seeing the business opportunity, Warren Woods and his sons bought 136 acres at the foot of Battle Mountain. They divided the land into lots, or "gold mines," in January 1893, named the town Victor, and sold the lots to eager prospectors and businessmen who not only dug mines but also built stores, saloons, and other businesses on the land.

In 1894 the Florence and Cripple Creek Railroad arrived, and the Victor Hotel was built to accommodate new visitors. Even when digging out the foundations a gold seam was discovered—this was to lead to the rich Gold Coin Mine (the hotel was moved to another lot). Victor is estimated to have produced almost $434 million worth of gold from over 500 local gold mines during the boom years. When the gold started to run out in 1900, thousands of miners moved on, and Victor declined. By the 1970s, the population was in the low hundreds, but gold mining restarted in 1976 with the Cripple Creek and Victor Gold Mining Company reprocessing the tailings. In 1994, the company opened the Cresson Mine a few miles north of Victor as the district's first large-scale open-pit mine. It produces a little over 10 tons of gold a year. Present-day Victor still reserves the authentic air of an 1890s mining town. Over two miles of mining tunnels remain under the town.

A fire engine in Victor (Teller County) in front of the town's city hall, c. 1910.

...he building still exists and is now shared with the police department.

View of Victor (Teller County), showing houses, businesses, and streets, taken between 1940 and 1945.

The population of Victor has been declining over the past hundred years from around 5,000 in 1900 to less than 500 today.

PUEBLO

The town started as Fort Pueblo in 1842 at the confluence of the Arkansas River and Fountain Creek as a collection of adobe structures beside what was then the U.S.-Mexico border. Local records suggest that the fort was attacked in December 1854 by Ute and Jacarilla Apache when they allegedly killed 19 men and a woman and captured two children. The trading post was then abandoned but revived in 1858–59 during the Colorado gold rush.

In the early days, Pueblo comprised four towns: Pueblo, South Pueblo, Central Pueblo, and Bessemer; the first three came together as Pueblo in 1886 with the latter joining in 1894. Pueblo rapidly became economically and socially important in Colorado.

The greatest disaster in the town's history was the Great Flood of 1921, caused by a cloudburst over the Arkansas River ten miles west and upstream of Pueblo. This was compounded when Fountain Creek flooded 30 miles north; the two floods met and merged at Pueblo. 1,500 people died, and $20 million worth of damage was done, with almost all of the riverside area destroyed, and the train tracks washed away. All the bridges over Fountain Creek were destroyed although those over the Arkansas held firm.

Pueblo became known as "Steel City" for its position as one of the biggest steel producing cities in the U.S. Pueblo is also the home of many electronics and aviation companies. In 1993, Congress recognized Pueblo as the "Home of Heroes" in honor of its four Medal of Honor recipients, more per capita than any other city in the U.S.

View of North Main Street in Pueblo (Pueblo County) shows a commercial street lined with multistory brick and stone buildings (including the Pueblo Opera House) and two rows of street railway tracks in the center of street. Taken between 1910 and 1920.

The Opera House as can be seen in the picture to the left has been demolished and replaced by this four-story office building. To its right still stands the historic federal building at 421 North Main Street.

View of a busy Main Street in Pueblo (Pueblo County) shows pedestrians, parked cars, and trolley car. The photo was taken between 1915 and 1925.

The magnificent six-story First National Bank of Pueblo remains completely intact and now houses a branch of the US Bank.

TRINIDAD

With occasional raids from Ute Indians, Trinidad was a lawless and rough frontier outpost. In 1867, the Christmas Day War broke out between Hispanics and Anglos, instigated by heavy drinking and boredom, bullets were fired, and the standoff became a truce the following day. But the local militia at Forts Worth and Reynolds were told war had broken out, so martial war was declared and troops dispatched to Trinidad. The bitterly cold weather—blizzards and -26°F—meant the trouble fizzled out.

In the early 1870s, gold was found in the Spanish Peaks, and about 60 mine shafts were dug, but the strike proved short lived. Trinidad was by then a useful resting place, and virtually every day up to 500 head of wagon-train oxen would be grazing outside the town preparing for the journey over Raton Pass—the hardest part of the Santa Fe Trail—while the freighters and cowboys visited the town's saloons and brothels.

In 1878, the Atchison, Topeka, and Santa Fe Railroad arrived at Trinidad, which by now had the reputation of being one of the roughest towns in the West lawman, gambler, and Western legend Bat Masterson was hired as town marshal to clean up Trinidad in 1882. With his reputation as a deadly shot, he never even had to draw his gun while here. His friends the Earp brothers and Doc Holliday joined him for a time straight after the shoot-out at the OK Corral in Arizona. Masterson left Trinidad in 1883. Trinidad become a commercial, agricultural, and coal mining center.

View of Commercial Street in Trinidad (Las Animas County), between 1890 and 1900.

The building that used to be the home of the Sears Dentist is now Lori Lyn's gift store, with a wide selection of greeting cards and Trinidad souvenirs.

View of the c.1900 Columbian Hotel and First National Bank on Main Street in Trinidad (Las Animas County).

The former headquarters of the Trinidad National Bank and Columbian Hotel retains its elegance, and is now home to a variety of shops.

PAGOSA SPRINGS

The small town of Pagosa Springs in Archuleta County is surrounded by the San Juan National Forest and the Southern Ute Indian lands in the southwest Four Corners region. The name is taken from *pah gosah*, a term which has been variously translated in recent years as meaning "boiling water" or "healing water." This part of Colorado was overlooked by the early Spanish settlers, and the first documented record of Pagosa was in 1859 when Captain J.N. McComb and his party explored the region. They camped at Pagosa Hot Springs, where it was noted that local Ute Indians revered the sulphur-rich waters and that "there is scarcely a more beautiful place." In 1867, Pagosa Springs became the site of Fort Lewis, built to control the troublesome Utes. For access, a military road was built across Elwood Pass. A few settlers, enough to justify a small post office, were already living near the hot springs. The nearby Ute reservation was dissolved in 1880, and the Indians moved elsewhere after the Meeker Massacre (1879). Fort Lewis was moved the following year to La Plata Mountains. In 1885, the town started to grow with settlers earning their living from coal mining, lumbering, and ranching.

In October 1900, a new railroad route opened between the sawmill at Pagosa Junction and the Denver and Rio Grande Railroad 31 miles away. Operated by the Rio Grande, Pagosa, and Northern Railroad, it was used by logging companies. The RGP&NRR collapsed in 1911, and after a few years, the D&RG took over the running. The Pagosa line was abandoned and the track was dismantled in 1936.

PAGOSA HOT SPRING, Archuleta County, Colo. Largest Hot Spring in the World—50x75 feet, no bottom. Steam from it in cool weather can be seen 25 miles distant. Temperature 140 degrees. Elevation 7,000 feet.

Men, women, and children gather around the edge of a large hot spring pool at Pagosa Springs (Archuleta County), c. 1890.

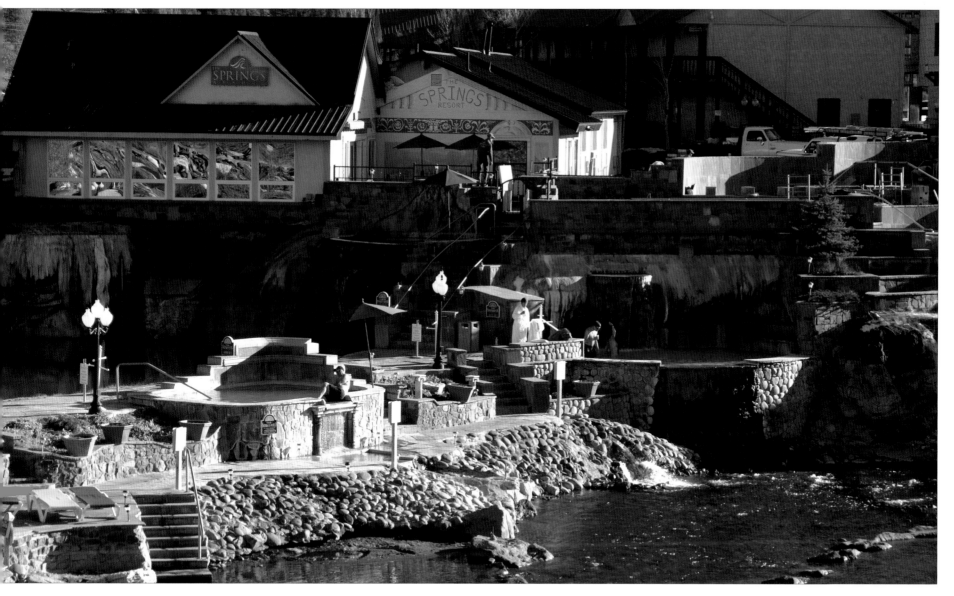

The Pagosa Springs resort is today a very popular tourist destination. The Ute Indians called it "Pah gosah," a term which has been variously translated as meaning "boiling water" or "healing water."

View of Main Street in Pagosa Springs (Archuleta County) shows commercial store fronts with awnings, pedestrians, and a parked cart, c. 1900.

Main Street today bears little resemblance to its 1900 counterpart. As in many a frontier town, buildings were wooden and a fire in one building would rapidly spread and destroy the entire street.

FOUR CORNERS NATIONAL MONUMENT

Four Corners National Monument is the only place in the entire United States where it is possible to stand in four different states simultaneously: in southeast Utah, southwest Colorado, northwest New Mexico, and northeast Arizona. The Navajo Nation and the Ute Mountain Indian Reservation also have their boundary here. The monument lies on the high Colorado Plateau in the middle of the Navajo Indian Reservation and is looked after by the Navajo Nation Department of Parks and Recreation. The monument was erected in 1912, at which time it was a simple cement block. This was replaced in 1992 with a much more impressive huge granite slab embedded with a large circular bronze disk which shows the exact four corners—the quadripoint—itself. The precise location is 36°59'56.31532"N 109°02'42.62019"W; the position was located by the Cadastral Survey, which performs legal boundary surveys for the federal government.

The Four Corners area became the property of the United States under the treaty following the Mexican-American War of 1848. However, the area was not fully surveyed by the U.S. government until 1868 when accurate mapping was required for the state of Colorado to be delineated. The Four Corners was established as the jurisdictional boundary in 1901 when the boundaries of Arizona Territory were demarcated. The Four Corners area includes a number of protected areas: Canyon de Chelly National Monument, Mesa Verde National Park, Hovenweep National Monument, and Monument Valley.

MESA VERDE

The Mesa Verde cliff dwellings were carved out of the rocks by the ancestral Pueblo peoples between AD 600 and 1300. In Mesa Verde National Park, there are over 4,700 archaeological sites, and 600 remarkably well-preserved cliff dwellings. Mesa Verde National Park was established by President Theodore Roosevelt in June 1906 to "preserve the works of man." Part of the National Park System, it covers over 81 square miles of federal land. The ancestral Puebloans (Anasazi) lived here for 700 years building elaborate stone homes within the sheltered alcoves of the canyon walls. The earliest inhabitants were the Basketmakers (AD 1-400); they made beautiful baskets but did not build homes or make pottery. No sites can be identified with this culture. Around 400, the first roofed dwellings were built and the people began to make pottery; they are known as Modified Basketmakers (400–750). In about 750, the houses started to be grouped together into compact pueblos by Developmental Pueblo peoples (750–1000). The buildings were made out of mud, clay, stones, poles, and layered masonry in a compact cluster surrounding an open court, in the center of which was dug a pit house. Over the years, the pit houses got deeper and deeper until they developed into the ceremonial rooms known as kivas. Finally in the 1200s, and not long before the communities disappeared, some people carved out the near-inaccessible sandstone and adobe cliff dwellings in alcoves high up the canyon walls (Classic Pueblo Period, 1100–1300).

Men climb over rocks in Cliff Canyon near Mesa Verde National Park (Montezuma County), 1892.

Men pose in Cliff Palace, a Native American (Anasazi) cliff dwelling ruin at Mesa Verde National Park, c. 1882.

CORTEZ

The sandy red soil of the Montezuma Valley looked ideal for growing crops if only there were any water—accordingly, in the late 19th century, the Montezuma Valley Water Supply Company was formed to develop the project. On land owned by the company's president, J.W. Hanna, the town plan for Cortez was laid out by the company's engineer, M.J. Mack, to provide houses for the hundreds of men needed to cut out the complicated network of tunnels, irrigation ditches, and laterals needed to divert water from the Dolores River into Montezuma Valley. By spring 1887 hundreds of men were working on the project.

A substantial town grew up, and the irrigation system meant that local farmers were able to grow abundant crops of alfalfa, wheat, potatoes, and apples. Soon labor and supplies for the surrounding area were channeled through Cortez; until in 1911, disaster struck and violent storms obliterated much of the irrigation system. The following years got worse with blistering summers, droughts and flu epidemics, and industries and businesses in general suffered a decline. Throughout the 1920s, the town population shrank as people left, but within a few years, new settlers escaping the dust bowl started to arrive. By the 1930s, the dairy industry was booming, gas was discovered nearby, and rainy seasons arrived, all encouraging town growth. The 1950s was a boom time for Cortez as nearby oil was found, and U.S. Highway 160 linked the town to the outside world. Tourism, especially to nearby Mesa Verde National Park, Monument Valley, and Four Corners, helped improve town finances.

View of Main Street in Cortez (Montezuma County) shows men, a horse-drawn wagon, a car, boardwalks, storefronts, and ashlar stone office buildings with entablature and balustrades, c. 1920.

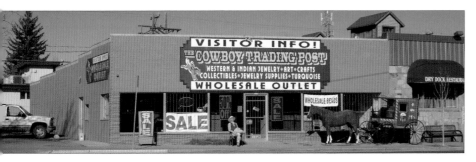

The RR Smith store (built in 1889) on the left and the building that housed the First National Bank still exist today.

View of Cortez (Montezuma County); sleeping Ute Mountain can be seen in the background, c. 1920.

This building housed a drug, hardware, and grocery store, and is now home to the Cortez Cultural Center.

DURANGO

Situated in La Plata County, Durango started as a railway town in 1880. The land was originally occupied by the Anasazi Indians, but they left the area around 1300.

The Denver and Rio Grande Railroad was built to serve the San Juan mining district and chose the site down the Animas River Valley for their depot and called it Durango. The railroad arrived in August 1881, and construction of the line to Silverton started a couple of months later. When the price of silver dropped from $1.05 an ounce to $0.63 an ounce in 1893, large mines in the Silverton district were forced to shut.

In summer 1889, a fire damaged seven blocks in the center of town; a new city ordinance stipulated that future buildings should be constructed from brick and stone. Throughout the 1880s, Durango served as the base for mining operations in Silverton, for which the Durango and Silverton Narrow Gauge Railroad was built. The steam railway that ran between Durango and the mining town of Silverton still runs today as a visitor attraction using the original early rolling stock; the narrow gauge is 36 inches apart instead of the standard gauge 56 inches apart. In 1918, 10 percent of the population died in six weeks in the devastating Spanish flu epidemic; additionally, the Gold King Mine closed, the Sunnyside Mine closed (but reopened 10 years later), and the Silverton Railroad closed.

Modern Durango is the largest town in southwest Colorado and is an ideal vacation destination for people wanting to visit Mesa Verde National Park and Ute Mountain Tribal Park.

A boy poses on a burro cart on a dirt street in Durango (La Plata County).

Main Street in Durango with an old-fashioned trolley bus run by Durango Transit.

SILVERTON

By 1875, around 100 settlers lived permanently in Silverton, and all the necessary businesses needed by a small town opened up: liquor store, blacksmith, newspaper, post office, etc., and of course an assay office. Within a year, the population had risen to 500, but life was hard, as the local cemetery ledger shows: 117 died in avalanches, 143 from consumption, 161 from pneumonia, 138 from influenza (mostly in the 1918 epidemic), and 202 from mine accidents.

Access to Silverton became easier in 1879 when the 12,590-foot-high Stony Pass wagon trail opened. Even better, three years later the Durango and Silverton Narrow Gauge Railroad arrived, and in 1884, a toll road opened between Silverton and Ouray. Silverton mines were at their peak between 1900 and 1912, and the population of the surrounding area topped 5,000. Four railroads competed for business, and over 30 mills and three smelters worked the ores brought down from the mountains. Most of the miners lived in boardinghouses up near the mines and only came to Silverton for the saloons and brothels. Churches and hotels were built, dancing was popular, and fraternal lodges and other clubs and associations appeared. In 1900, many civic buildings were constructed, including a town hall, a courthouse, and jail. Utility services like water pipes and sewers were laid down, sidewalks installed, and electricity appeared. After the boom of the silver years, most of the miners departed and many of the mines closed. The last big mine, the Sunnyside, closed in the early 1990s. The town's population is now a little over 500.

Women and girls play baseball in the dirt street in front of a two-story brick school building with a mansard roof and cupola in Silverton (San Juan County), 1884.

The San Juan County Courthouse was built in 1907 at a cost of $79,000.

View of the town of Silverton (San Juan County), with the Animas River and Kendall and Sultan mountains in the distance, c. 1890.

similar view of the town today shows that it has not expanded over the last hundred years. Settled in 1874, Silverton saw its population eventually rise to around 5,000; the current population is only around 500.

TELLURIDE

Telluride was formally founded in 1887 and named after tellurium, a metalloid element found in the nearby mountains alongside the gold, copper, silver, lead, and zinc.

Isolated Telluride remained a small settlement until a toll road opened in 1881; this made the town more accessible and allowed wagons to roll where only pack mules could work before. In June 1889, the San Miguel Valley Bank in Telluride was robbed of $24,580 by Butch Cassidy in his first big recorded crime. More welcome was the Rio Grande Southern Railroad in 1890, which brought in thousands of foreign immigrants; more mines opened and more gold ore was transported, and Telluride became a fully fledged mining town. Between 1905 and 1911, the district produced over $16 million worth of gold and silver.

In common with other mining towns at the turn of the 20th century, Telluride suffered through the Colorado Labor Wars. The mines ran continuously, with miners working up to 12 hours a day in dangerous conditions. After violent clashes, agreement was reached: for an eight-hour day, most miners were paid $3.

Mining declined through the 20th century, to be replaced in the 1960s by a much younger generation who came for the outdoor life and casual lifestyle. In 1972, the first ski lift was installed, and skiing took over to become the biggest business in town. The newcomers also started numerous music and film festivals for which Telluride has become famous.

Snowcapped peaks and spots of golden autumn color greet visitors to the San Juan Skyway.

Autumn scene from the San Juan Mountains.

MONTROSE

The small town of Montrose lies in Uncompahgre Valley on the western side of the Continental Divide. It was named by Joseph Selig after a character in *The Legends of Montrose* by Sir Walter Scott, because the area reminded him of the Scottish lochs.

The town's initial role was to supply the nearby mining communities, but when the ores ran out, the businesses turned to agriculture as the fertile valley soils produced vegetables, fruits, and grains as well as providing pasture for livestock. In 1882, the narrow-gauge Denver and Rio Grande Railroad arrived from Denver, bringing with it business and change. Montrose grew into a rough frontier cow town, rail stop, and freight hub as well as a thriving business center for the mining industry, especially after a narrow-gauge branch line was built to serve the mines and camps of the San Juan Mountains. However, water was scarce until 1909, when the seven-mile-long Gunnison Tunnel opened to channel irrigation water from the Gunnison River in the Black Canyon to Uncompahgre Valley. In September 1909, President William Howard Taft came to Montrose to dedicate the project; the irrigation water turned the fertile valley into valuable agricultural land and began a new era of prosperity.

Agriculture is still an important business, and Montrose remains a hub for agriculture, general commerce, and transport. Today, hunters, anglers, and various outdoor enthusiasts use Montrose as their base for Gunnison National Park and the Black Canyon, as well as for winter skiing in the San Juan Mountains.

The Colorado Potato Growers Exchange was formed in 1923 to regulate the marketing of potatoes. Twenty separate groups banded together as a central statewide agency. They stabilized the market so effectively that it later added onions (1928) and pinto beans (1968) to its operations.

Montrose Regional Airport has two runways. The airport is served year-round by United Express (operated by Skywest) to Denver. Summer service is provided by Continental Airlines to Houston. Winter service expands to Houston and Newark with Continental Airlines, to Dallas and Chicago with American Airlines, and to Atlanta and Salt Lake City with Delta Airlines.

GRAND JUNCTION

Located at the junction of the Colorado River (originally the Grand River) and the Gunnison River, Grand Junction sits between three important geological features: to the northwest are the Bookcliffs, east is the Grand Mesa, and southwest lies Colorado National Monument. When Colorado became a state in 1876, pioneers arrived in the valley and soon violent clashes between the Ute and the settlers were commonplace. Following the Meeker Massacre and the Battle of Milk Creek, the U.S. government forced the last Ute off their land and onto reservations in northeast Utah and southwest Colorado in September 1881. Immediately, even more settlers arrived, including George A. Crawford, the founder of Grand Junction. In June 1882, the city of Grand Junction was officially established, and within five months, the Denver and Rio Grande Western Railroad started construction at Grand Junction. Connecting the city to Denver and Gunnison, the railroad increased prosperity and was soon the biggest employer. By 1900, Grand Junction had grown into a regular frontier town with all the businesses and services necessary for a busy, largely agricultural community—canning factories, sugar manufacturers, stockyards, and so on. Irrigation projects using water from the Grand Mesa and the Colorado River were initiated to supply the town and the dry but fertile soils of the valley with water.

Present-day Grand Junction is important for gas and oil and is a major commercial and transportation hub for the entire area, but agriculture, especially fruit, remains preeminent.

Grand Junction is the largest city in western Colorado. According to 2007 estimates, the population of the city is 53,662.

he view of Grand Junction from Colorado National Monument. Established in 1911 by President William Taft, Colorado National Monument preserves one of the grand landscapes of the American Vest. Sheer-walled canyons, towering monoliths, colorful formations, desert bighorn sheep, soaring eagles, and a spectacular road reflect the history of the plateau-and-canyon country.

RIFLE

The town of Rifle was founded in 1882 by Abram Maxfield near where Rifle Creek joins the Colorado River. Rifle lies in Garfield County in the plateau and canyon country of western Colorado. Historically, Rifle is a farming and ranching community, and present-day Rifle is the regional center of the cattle ranching industry.

The biggest mystery about the town is how it got its name. There are four explanations. The most popular comes from the late 19th century when a group of white trappers were working around the creek, and when they left, one of them had forgotten his rifle leaning against a tree, so giving the place its name; he apparently returned for his weapon. Another is that the town was named for its citizens' custom of using rifle fire to signal to each other. The third theory says that in 1880 a group of soldiers were working on the road between Meeker and the place that became Rifle. One of the soldiers left his rifle behind at the camp along the stream bank, and when he returned for it, he named the creek Rifle Creek and the town took its name from the creek. Yet another story says a surveyor lost his rifle here and named the place after it on his map. The surrounding mesas and mountains have always attracted hunters and trappers. In 1901, Theodore Roosevelt arrived here hunting for bears. Fourteen miles north of Rifle is Rifle Falls State Park, where the water falls over a spectacular limestone cliff. In 1910, the townspeople of Rifle built the Rifle Hydroelectric Plant here to make use of the falls. This changed the natural fall of the waters from one wide waterfall into the three falls seen today.

The Grand Hogback, a striking geologic feature, is a vast monocline bordering the White River Plateau and the Colorado River Valley. Measuring 70 miles long, it is an S-shaped spine of Mesa Verde formation sandstone flanked by steep, deeply incised ridges.

ifle Gap Dam is about 5½ miles north of Rifle, at a point where Rifle Creek cuts through the Grand Hogback. The dam is an earth-fill structure with a spillway. Rifle Gap Reservoir has a total capacity f 13,602 acre-feet and an active capacity of 12,168 acre-feet, and when full, a surface area of 359 acres.

GLENWOOD SPRINGS

Settler and businessman Isaac Cooper wanted to make the settlement called Defiance a resort for enjoying the hot springs, but he was greatly hampered by its rough character. At his wife Sarah's suggestion (probably), Defiance was changed to Glenwood Springs in 1885 after Glenwood, Iowa, their hometown. The town plan was laid out, the first church was built, and two newspapers were established. By 1886, electricity lit the town, and a hydro-electric plant built. The following year, the First National Bank opened a branch, and in October, the Denver and Rio Grande Railroad arrived via Glenwood Canyon. In December the Colorado Midland Railroad also arrived, this time via the Roaring Fork and Frying Pan River valleys. Soon, Leadville and Aspen miners were using this new transport facility each weekend as "laundry trains" to bathe at the hot springs, do their laundry, and spend their money in the saloons and brothels.

Doc Holliday, the western outlaw and legend, spent his last months here in 1887 and was buried in Linwood Cemetery (a monument to him was erected in 1955 although the precise location of his grave is unknown).

With the miners long gone, the hot springs attracted a more gentile crowd, and Glenwood began to prosper. Glenwood Springs is a prime activity vacation center.

Theodore Roosevelt spent three weeks here in January 1901 when vice president, and returned again in 1905, as depicted in the three black-and-white pictures on the top row.

A view of Glenwood Springs (Garfield County) shows the Yampa Hot Springs and bathhouses, the Colorado River, railroad grades and bridges, wood frame houses, and commercial buildings, c. 1880.

This view of Glenwood Springs shows the famous hot springs bathhouses, which have retained a lot of their original architecture, and the main town on the other side of the Colorado River.

A group of young men stand on each other's shoulders beside a fountain in the Hot Springs Pool, Glenwood Springs (Garfield County), 1899.

The famous Glenwood Springs Spa of the Rockies still stands largely unchanged from the historic photo on the left.

ASPEN

Surrounded by mountains and wilderness on three sides, the remote town of Aspen was named for the number of aspen trees growing around the area. Aspen is the county seat of Pitkin County, and for many decades now has been an upscale ski resort and somewhat unconventional home for numerous celebrities, giving Aspen an enviable aura of glamour. This has raised house prices sky-high, even though many of them are only vacation homes.

Founded by miners as their camp at the end of Roaring Fork Valley during the Colorado silver boom in the winter of 1879, Aspen was originally called Ute City after the local Native American nation, but was renamed Aspen in 1880. For one year, between 1881 and 1882, more silver was mined in Aspen than anywhere else in Colorado. The Sherman Silver Purchase Act of 1890 doubled the government's obligation to buy silver, and accordingly Aspen's miners increased their production. The town grew with silver prosperity and by 1893 had grown to include a hospital, banks, two theaters, and an opera house, all lit by electric lights. Within weeks of President Cleveland repealing the Sherman Silver Purchase Act following the economic panic of 1893, the silver mines around Aspen started closing, and thousands of miners found themselves without work and were forced to leave town. Silver mining never recovered.

By 1930, Aspen was again a quiet backwater town with only 705 permanent residents. Many fine old buildings and residences were empty, and some businessmen started to think

View of Aspen (Pitkin County) from Aspen Mountain. Landmarks include the bell tower, firehouse, Wheeler Opera House, and the Hotel Jerome. Smuggler Mountain is in the distance, c. 1890.

Ski lifts run by the Aspen Skiing Corporation, which was formed in 1946, and the center of town, which is overlooked by some of the most expensive property in America.

of developing the skiing potential for visitors, but the project never got off the ground thanks to the interruption of World War II. Instead, the Aspen Skiing Corporation was founded in 1946, and Aspen rapidly became a popular destination. Other businesses grew with the popularity of the resort, and Aspen has never looked back.

The historic character of the city has been challenged in recent decades by skyrocketing property values and the proliferation of second homes, increasingly shutting low- and middle-income workers out of the city and creating a large pool of commuters from nearby bedroom communities such as Basalt and Carbondale. At the same time, in stark contrast to its historic character, the city has emerged into international fame as a glitzy playground of the wealthy and famous.

The downtown has been largely transformed into an upscale shopping district that includes high-end restaurants, salons, and boutiques. Aspen boasts a Chanel, Dior, Louis Vuitton, Prada, Gucci, Fendi, Tod's, and recently a Burberry boutique.

The booming real estate market has forced the city to struggle between permitting growth and restricting it. The city today remains a mix of high-end luxury homes and condos intermixed with legacy residences and mobile home parks populated by an old guard of Aspen residents struggling to maintain the unique character of the city. Aspen has become a second and third home to many international jet-setters.

A horse-drawn stagecoach is parked in front of the Hotel Jerome in Aspen (Pitkin County), c. 1890.

Jerome B. Wheeler, the co-owner of New York's Macy's Department Store, built the Hotel Jerome in 1889 to emulate great European hotels such as London's fabled Claridge's.

A Colorado Midland Railroad train passes over the East Maroon Creek Bridge near Aspen in Pitkin County, c. 1890.

The East Maroon Creek Bridge was converted to a motor vehicle bridge in 1929. The original supports still stand largely unchanged.

LEADVILLE

The city of Leadville was founded by the mine owners August Meyer and Horace Tabor in 1877. Claims could be made with as little as $37, and a few of the owners became millionaires overnight. It has been estimated that the Leadville district produced some 240 million ounces of silver, over 2.9 million ounces of gold, 1 million tons of lead, 785 tons of zinc, and 53,000 tons of copper. Within three years, Leadville had a population of over 40,000, was one of the biggest and most productive silver camps in the world, and inevitably, was a very dangerous and wild place. Many of the most notorious characters of the Wild West spent time in Leadville, including the Younger Gang, who actually lived here; Doc Holliday, who had his final shoot-out with Billy Allen here; the Earps were seen here, as was William "Bat" Masterson, journalist, frontiersman, and U.S. marshal. The silver boom lasted until the repeal of the Sherman Silver Purchase Act in 1893, and with the collapse, the fortunes and population of Leadville declined. Some miners still worked, but now most of the ore was lead and zinc.

During World War II, the U.S. Army Air Force built Leadville Army Airfield to the northwest of Leadville as an auxiliary field to Petersen Army Air Base in Colorado Springs, but it was abandoned after the war. Wartime mining of molybdenum (needed for high-strength steel alloys), which had been discovered in 1918 at the nearby Climax mine, was stepped up as wartime demand required; it closed in the 1980s. The town is now a visitor attraction both for its historic past and for its outdoor recreation.

View of the three-story brick Tabor Opera House on Harrison Avenue in Leadville (Lake County). A wooden passage connects the third story of the opera house with the Clarendon Hotel next door, c. 1880.

Built in 1879, the Tabor Opera House was acclaimed "the largest and best west of the Mississippi!" Today, the Tabor Opera House has plans for a full restoration to its previous days of glory.

View of Harrison Avenue in Leadville (Lake County), c. 1925.

eadville is the highest incorporated city in the United States. This former silver mining camp lies near the headwaters of the Arkansas River in the heart of the Rocky Mountains.

INDEX